# THE JOURNAL BOOK

CATHARINE BRAMKAMP

# CONTENTS

1. Why Journal? — 1
2. What is Transformative Writing? — 5
3. Health Benefits of Journaling — 11
4. Transformative Typing — 17
5. What Kind of Journal is Best? — 21
6. Set a Time limit — 30
7. Time — 33
8. Mind Maps and Timelines — 42
   Journal for Better Family Relationships — 47
9. Talk to the Dead — 50
10. What's Your Story? — 55
11. Your Passion Project — 59
12. Journal for creative mojo — 63
13. The Pain and Perils of Starting Over — 66
14. Making Mistakes, And Why We Should — 70
15. The Man in the Arena — 73
16. Pushing over the stack of creative blocks — 74
    Tech — 77
17. Travel Journals — 80
18. Beat the Holidays Blues — 85
19. How to Game Difficult Tasks — 91
    Acknowledgments — 95
    About the Author — 97
20. Books for and about Journaling — 98

Published by A Few Little Books
June 2020
Nevada City, CA
ISBN 978-0-9816848-4-0
All Rights Reserved

✺ Created with Vellum

# CONTENTS

1. Why Journal? — 1
2. What is Transformative Writing? — 5
3. Health Benefits of Journaling — 11
4. Transformative Typing — 17
5. What Kind of Journal is Best? — 21
6. Set a Time limit — 30
7. Time — 33
8. Mind Maps and Timelines — 42
   Journal for Better Family Relationships — 47
9. Talk to the Dead — 50
10. What's Your Story? — 55
11. Your Passion Project — 59
12. Journal for creative mojo — 63
13. The Pain and Perils of Starting Over — 66
14. Making Mistakes, And Why We Should — 70
15. The Man in the Arena — 73
16. Pushing over the stack of creative blocks — 74
    Tech — 77
17. Travel Journals — 80
18. Beat the Holidays Blues — 85
19. How to Game Difficult Tasks — 91
    Acknowledgments — 95
    About the Author — 97
20. Books for and about Journaling — 98

Published by A Few Little Books
June 2020
Nevada City, CA
ISBN 978-0-9816848-4-0
All Rights Reserved

✺ Created with Vellum

# 1
# WHY JOURNAL?

I've seen first-hand the transformation that writing - focused, purposeful writing - can do. If we all started our day with just ten minutes of reflection and intention, the world would be a kinder more tolerant place. We are all writers; we just need to get into the habit.

This journaling book is about the how. You will learn how to write, what to write and what kind of journal works best, and whether you need to handwrite, type, or talk.

This is about transformation because writing will change you, so it may as well change you for the better.

**Goals**

Writing down your goals automatically gives you a 70 percent higher chance of reaching them. What I love about journaling is it gives you space for more than merely listing the discrete steps towards a goal, it also provides space to ask why you are walking in that direction in the first place.

. . .

## STRESS

Write down all your complaints, stress, and anxiety before saying anything out loud. By taking the brunt of your frustrations, your journal can save relationships. Not only that, just expressing stress on paper will save your heart as well as your gut.

## CHANGE

Journal every day and pretty soon you will notice patterns of thinking, patterns of concern, repeat complaints. Transformative journaling will help break the complaint cycle and allow you to start solving your problems, all by writing it down.

## HISTORY

Keep a record. Journals are the building blocks of memoirs and novels. You may think your life isn't startling or important, you are wrong.

## LEARN

Want to remember what you've learned? Write it down. Just the act of taking notes will help secure that idea in your mind, even if you never review the notes again.

## GRATITUDE

If your family is tired of hearing you exclaim how grateful you are for the sun, the blue sky or the garbage pick-up (think of that, a stranger in a truck drives by every week and takes your trash away, what a marvelous invention!) write down your wonder. Journal about how you feel and what you love. Gush. When you are busy feeling and expressing gratitude, there is no room for fear or anger. But maybe just keep it in your journal.

### Creativity

Daily journaling enhances and attracts creativity. As we will discuss in the chapters on passion and creativity, the Muse makes appointments. If you show up every day, pretty soon she will too.

Two key gurus if you will, of the journaling world are Natalie Goldberg and Julia Cameron, there are more, but these two writers have influenced classes, book series, and books like this one, so they deserve a mention.

Natalie Goldberg's *Writing Down the Bones*, combines writing with Zen Buddhist practices often conflating the two. Published 1986 it was revolutionary and her mantra, keep writing no matter what, spawned countless classes, practices, writers and in my case, a master's thesis. *The Artist's Way*, published by Julia Cameron in 1992 furthered the idea of writing practice, creating art for health and sanity as well as writing for a specific time at a specific time of day. *The Artist Way* empire is formidable, but the subsequent books are pretty much the same rehash of the original theme of writing, not that I begrudge an author capitalizing on a good idea.

The essence of both author's approaches, seeped in two different decades (consider the audacity of discussing art during the 80s and 90s) is timed writing that draws straight from your subconscious, no chaser. To get what you want, you need to write around the conscious, editorial section of your brain so you can uncover and express greater truths and insights.

. . .

## SHARING IS NOT CARING

Journaling your truth and insights are exactly what you are going for but do know that all that marvelous juicy writing is not necessarily ready to be shared either with close family members (perhaps especially not family members) nor with the greater reading public. If you want to share your wonderful insights, do! But edit first. Maybe even edit second. Contrary to popular myth, even though Jack Kerouac (under the influence of Cassady, Ginsberg, Snyder, the tenants of automatic writing, plus too much alcohol) wrote *On The Road* more or less spontaneously, he edited the work before publication. Contrast Kerouac against Gertrude Stein who believed every word that poured from her subconscious was publication worthy. Who are we still reading? Yeah. Write your truth, be spontaneous but don't think it is ready to drop into your blog. It's not. And that is more than okay. Managing and smoothing your writing is a much later activity. We are just discussing how to first to get it all down, just for you.

## 2
## WHAT IS TRANSFORMATIVE WRITING?

Transformative writing is intentional writing to invoke change and increase well-being. Shaun McNiff a leading scholar on the expressive arts (and author of a most helpful book *Trust the Process*), helps define the essence of transformative writing, "Words become agents of transformation, shamanic horses that carry expression and transport people to change."

Numerous scientific studies by James W. Pennebaker and other scientists have shown that writing affects heart rate, blood pressure, and the immune system. The power of writing from the heart results in stress reduction and the restoration of emotional equilibrium. Are there graphs and double-blind studies? No, just results.

"I saw the angel in the marble and carved till I set him free." - Michelangelo.

"So has each author wielded the pen to liberate the creative spirit within. Each writer has discovered that words have the power to call upon angels and banish demons. Through writing, the self recognizes its identity with greater definition, harvests its wisdom, and wrestles with challenges, transforming them into building blocks of growth." - Pennebaker.

Writing and journaling is building, you will build on ideas, you will build using forms. You will build a better life. You can start right now or pick up where you may have left off years ago.

Remember our first journals? We wrote when we were sad, we wrote when we were happy, we often complained about the food. We wrote endlessly about our size, our hair, our tan lines and how none measured up because at the time, not being in vogue was a terrible tragedy. With a little perspective and years of journaling, and not a few cocktails with our best friends, we realize that no one felt in vogue and no one felt perfect. With those revelations in mind, during our last move, I cheerfully recycled years of teen journals. The poetry was bad, the complaints were monotonous, and the song lyrics were (appropriately) maudlin. The only thing I got right was my wishful description of the perfect man: tall, dark, handsome with glasses who happened to be brilliant.

Nailed it.

What I did not do or create in those early years was any kind of tangible, reportable change. Journaling helped get me through the years, but I don't believe I necessarily, consciously progressed, I simply outgrew the angst.

You, on the other hand, don't need to wait to outgrow your angst.

### Make it Better

If you've been journaling forever, switch up your writing from just griping and complaining to exploring how you can make the situation better or how you can think about your situation differently.

The transformative part comes when you start expressing what you want to happen. There are benefits to bitching, there are more benefits to moving your brain and your consciousness to a more positive place leaving you with little, in the long run, to complain about.

Since thoughts create our reality it makes sense that the more often you think and interpret the world in one way, the world will increasingly appear to you in that same way. Think sad drizzly thoughts all day, and pretty soon you'll cry every time you see cloud.

How to switch it up? Fortunately, it's not about willpower or just "change your mind" Or "flip the switch." I've always found it difficult to just change, or as my helpful husband mocks - stop feeling that way (!). What works best is steady improvement, habit and incremental change.

Here is how to do it. (I know, right in the first chapter!)

1. Get up.
2. Secure the hot or cold morning beverage of choice. This is not the moment to try a new beverage, or to create the world's most healthy smoothie, that is just an excuse to put off writing. Grab the coffee or tea and pull out your computer or journal (we will discuss these in detail in a later chapter).
3. Write for ten minutes or until you've filled three pages.
4. Go about your day.

That's it.

From that daily practice all sorts of benefits, ideas and insights will arise. All you need to do it start.

Caution: *The side effects of journaling is a marked decrease in drama coupled with a significant reduction in screaming, crying and tantrums. If, after working through this book, you miss the daily hysterics, you are welcome to quit journaling and return to your previous stress filled days with my blessing.*

## Plasticity - not the stuff floating in the ocean

REMEMBER JACK KEROUAC, fan of automatic writing? Here is a couple of what he calls essentials from his *Belief and Technique for Modern Prose*

"Scribbled secret notebooks, and wild typewritten pages, for yr own joy."

"Keep track of every day the date emblazoned in yr writing"

"Mental State. If possible write "without consciousness" in semi trance […] allowing subconscious to admit in own uninhibited interesting necessary and so "modern" language what conscious art would censor, and write excitedly, swiftly, with writing-or-typing-cramps."

Yesterday, you rose, you drank, you wrote. So what? The what is that you are now on your way to changing your thoughts, your reality and your brain. How does writing change the brain?

### YOUR BRAIN

For a brief time, the last 4,000 years, it was thought that the brain did not change or grow after adolescence. The Egyptians didn't think the brain was worth much at all, certain that all thought, and emotion centered from the heart. Familiar with the concepts of a heavy heart and having a heart as light as a feather? Egyptian. During mummification, priests preserved the heart, but sucked out the brain and tossed it.

Just for perspective.

Fast forward in scientific discoveries. Scientists researching stroke recovery, discover that contrary to previous beliefs that the brain stops growing in our early twenties, it can, in fact rewire and improve at any age. Scientists studied recovering stroke patients and saw, with surprise, that brain synapses grew and reworked around the stroke damaged brain sections and changed to take on new jobs and form new connections. Not only can the human brain grow and develop at any point in our lives, but we can also learn and form new critical brain synapses at any time. In fact, learning was abruptly seen as not only desirable but important (even critical) to maintaining health and quality of life.

Initially, this new exciting research measured the growth of brain function based on facility with puzzles. It was thought that seniors who completed countless crossword puzzles or number puzzles like Sudoku would keep their brains flexible and benefit from a higher functionality. Working on puzzles like crossword or math grids became a thing, a way to keep your mind from slipping into the grim dark netherland of Alzheimer's. But for me, it was bad news. I had no desire to spend my golden years filing in endless crosswords. I don't even like Words with Friends. Clearly without the daily exercise of the NYT crossword, the goal of which is to fill in using a ball point pen, I was doomed to aging ungracefully and ending my days a little daft (or, with enough money, eccentric).

A few years later science helped me out. It was discovered that all those sincere and busy seniors diligently working their math puzzles accomplished was - becoming more adept at Sudoku. Working on puzzles made you much better at puzzles, but not much else. The puzzles just grew and strengthened the puzzle synapse (roughly, I'm paraphrasing years of research).

Enter, journaling and writing. While practicing puzzles begat better puzzle efficacy, journaling and writing actually begat better overall brain function. You certainly get better at writing, but the writing also helps with memory, health, mood.

If you, like me, are a fan of bias confirmation, this new information is welcome indeed. For those of us who have spent our entire life scribbling in journals alternatively hating our hair, our thighs and X, this is a delightful discovery: what we are already doing is actually good for us.

This almost never happens.

If you want your life to change, you can't write just anything, you must be focused. While you will start with recording random thoughts and impressions, your journaling will evolve to be more intentional, or transformational. Focused writing will not only improve your brain plasticity, as much or more than crossword and Sudoku puzzles, it will improve your life right now.

Journaling about X won't change X. But journaling can change how you think about X and how you will handle X in the future. In other words, don't complain about X, solve for X.

Just by writing down what you really want, what would be lovely to experience and what would make you happy, you change your focus. Writing actually trains your subconscious to create solutions. After writing for a few weeks you'll discover that instead of recording what sucks, you'll start writing about a better solution. Trite, I know, but it actually works. But only if you want your life to improve.

I like to say that changing your story can change your life. Transformative journaling is one of the best ways to do it.

## 3
## HEALTH BENEFITS OF JOURNALING

Journaling is good for us.
Like coffee.
Like red wine.
It's enough to make you believe in a benevolent god.

The science on the health benefits of journaling is not conclusive because reports of well-being, are difficult to definitively measure. But according to programs like *Journal on Line*, consistent journaling can:

- Boost thinking ability
- Increase working memory
- Reduce pain, tension, and fatigue
- Enhance mood and sleep quality
- Positively influence immune system function
- Help wounds heal more quickly
- Reduce doctor visits
- Better grades in school

- Faster hiring to a new job
- Lower your stress hormones
- Decrease blood pressure
- Improve problem-solving
- Reduce symptoms from some chronic illnesses

WRITING HAS ALWAYS BEEN a part of traditional therapy. For years, practitioners have used logs, questionnaires, journals and other writing forms to help people heal from stresses and traumas.

New research suggests expressive writing may also offer physical benefits to people battling terminal or life-threatening diseases. Studies by those in the forefront of this research--psychologists James Pennebaker, PhD, of the University of Texas at Austin, and Joshua Smyth, PhD, of Syracuse University--suggest that writing about emotions and stress can boost immune functioning in patients with such illnesses as HIV/AIDS, asthma and arthritis.

Of course, it can be argued that other factors, such as changes in social support, or simply time, could instead be the real health aids. But an intensive research review by Smyth, published in 1998 in the Journal of Consulting and Clinical Psychology (Vol. 66, No. 1), suggests that writing does make a difference, though the degree of difference depends on the population being studied and the form that writing takes.

Researchers are only beginning to understand and define why writing may benefit the immune system, and why some people appear to benefit more than others. There is emerging agreement, however, that the key to writing's effectiveness is in the way people use it to interpret their experiences, right down to the words they choose. Venting emotions alone--

whether through writing or talking--is not enough to relieve stress, and thereby improve health. Smyth emphasizes that in order to tap writing's healing power, people must use it to better understand and learn from their emotions.

PENNEBAKER CONCLUDED that the enlightenment that can occur through such writing compares with the benefits of verbal guided exploration in psychodynamic psychotherapies. For example, even talking into a tape recorder has shown positive health effects. The curative mechanism appears to be relief of the stress that exacerbates disease, researchers believe. (Bridget Murray, Monitor)

Even if the results and benefits of writing is difficult for scientists to codify, if we can actually manage our health using a drug-free technique like daily journaling, why not?

### PRACTICE WITHOUT PERFECTION

Journaling is a practice, like Zen, like yoga, like music. And like those wonderful practices, once you are hooked, you can and will continue for the rest of your life. Journaling is very much in these practice categories. There is no finish, but there is improvement.

How to approach journaling? Fortunately, you do not need to travel to a gym or studio to journal. Unfortunately, you don't have many excuses. You can journal anywhere, but more specifically, it's easy to journal at home.

### JOURNAL for your health

If your goal is to gain and maintain better health, your journal can be an important partner. Journal about what you want right now: breathe easier, feel lighter, walk faster.

Journal about the future and describe what your life will be like once your health or recovery goals are achieved. Create and list goals that move you and get you excited. The bigger and more interesting the goal, the more likely you are to make the immediate sacrifices, like physical therapy or giving up a delicious food, to get there.

A friend almost died in a horrific bus accident in Laos. She was told she would never walk again. Not one for following orders, she was not only determined to fully recover from her injuries, she set the goal that in one year she would circumvent Everest, then a year after that, she would climb the damn thing.

Talk about goals. With each supervised, faltering step, she kept Everest in her mind. She stayed focused on her goal: circumvent, climb.

Long story short because she did write a book about it - she did both. On time.

What is the big picture for you? What do you want to do and how will you feel when you accomplish it?

Journaling helps us get past our current situation and into the habit of visualizing something better, something bigger or more interesting than our present circumstance. What is your own personal goal? Putting your head on your knees in yoga class? Running a marathon? Climbing Mt. Fuji or Kilimanjaro? What other interesting outcomes or side benefits may happen because you kept your eye on the goal?

Will you be able to hike around Sicily once that new knee is working perfectly? Once the chemo is complete will you buy a new convertible because the wind won't mess your hair?

Create a finish line and for God's sake when you reach it - follow through, otherwise your subconscious as well as your Muse will never trust you again.

There many books focused on using writing to manage

your weight, even Julia Cameron repurposed her Artist Way book into a diet book *The Writing Diet: Write Yourself Right-Sized.* (I said it was a (ahem) large franchise).

Since I've used writing to help my diets (yes, plural, begging the question why, if I don't like to diet, do I diet so often which then begs the question of why is wine so darn delicious?) I can address how to start the process.

I start big, in every way. I write about how I will feel after losing the weight (about 30 pounds for those of you playing the home game). I write down the short- and long-term goals: this many pounds, this kind of food. But I also discovered that more specific markers were even more effective. I wanted to fit back into my engagement ring and birthday rings that had grown too tight (sure, blame the rings). I wanted to wear an old investment piece that dry cleaning had shrunk. I wanted to put my head on my knees in yoga. I want to climb the hills leading to my mountain home without losing my breath. Those immediate and tangible goals were a far better incentive than creating a depressing list of forbidden foods.

*Lose weight* is a terrible goal. What do you do with that? It's like all those general, vague New Year's Resolutions - be nicer, be successful, be stronger. And while we are asking questions and transforming our health, why are you losing weight, or walking faster or putting your head on your knees? Journaling allows us to spend quality time asking those questions. Journaling encourages us to pull out all species of assumptions and examine their roots. Better questions will lead to far better answers. A strong why can help you reach that goal faster than just a vague statement of general purpose.

. . .

Since we've recently worked through rather anxious times, and anxiety can trigger all sorts of health issues along with inappropriate responses, like an uncontrollable desire to eat the whole bag of Nacho Cheese Chips, something science is reluctant to explain, Journaling, as you can imagine, helps alleviate some if not most of our anxiety, both natural and inflicted. Plus, journal writing doesn't stain your fingers orange.

**Journaling helps with anxiety by:**

- Calming and clearing your mind
- Releasing pent-up feelings and everyday stress
- Letting go of negative thoughts
- Exploring your experiences with anxiety
- Writing about your struggles and your successes
- Enhancing your self-awareness
- Recording and understanding triggers
- Tracking your progress as you undergo health treatments

Journaling will make you feel better. Track weight, celebrate health goals, write out anxious thoughts and terrors, journaling will help it all. All for the low, low entry price of pen and paper.

## 4
## TRANSFORMATIVE TYPING

Which is better, in transformative terms, typing into a computer or on-line program, voice recording while doing something else, or handwriting into a journal, or onto a page?

Handwriting. Thought I'd save you some reading time.

Handwriting facilitates the direct connection between heart and hand and is the best, fastest way to help transform your thoughts and re-wire your brain. Writing by hand forces you to slow down and welcome slow burning ideas welling up from your heart and gut. How delicious is this? Who would believe that slower work engenders faster results?

In the New York Times, one Yale psychologist commented that "with handwriting, the very act of putting it down forces you to focus on what's important." Citing a study published in *Developmental Neuropsychology*, the Times reported:

Printing, cursive writing, and typing on a keyboard are all associated with distinct and separate brain patterns — and each result in a distinct end product. When the children composed text by hand, they not only consistently produced more words more quickly than they did on a keyboard but expressed more ideas.

WRITING by hand requires more subtle and complicated motion from your fingers than typing as well as actually increasing activity in the brain's motor cortex, an effect that's similar to meditation. This explains why journaling can feel therapeutic and why it helps with mindfulness.

## VOICE RECORDING

I've encountered a few writers who brag that they dictate all their work into their phone while walking around town. They then send the audio recording to be transcribed (paying the transcriber a lot of money to do so). Once the work is transcribed, the author declares the work is perfect and fires the whole missive off to the publishers.

I too want to believe in unicorns.

Let's imagine for a minute that it is actually possible to dictate a perfect book. Great. The work may claim the official number of pages, but the work is based solely on what comes through the head, not the heart, not the body. Great work, even decent, readable work, wells up from your heart, your gut, your very cells, and of course, from your soul. Remember the ancient Egyptians threw away the brain while favoring every other major organ. How you capture and record your creative ideas matters. And how you capture your emotions and thoughts in order to change them and transform your life, really matters.

Writing is a mind/body exercise, worth making, worth keeping in shape.

Do use voice recording for notes and ideas, especially if you are driving. Speaking out your thoughts does have benefits. But transcribing those recordings yourself has further benefits. Speak, but schedule time to transcribe your notes so you get the benefits of writing out your good ideas. And please, even in the face of first thought, best thought, no one said anything about first thought, publishable thought.

### Restless movement

I love teaching live classes because I get feedback on information or ideas, I was unaware of. One afternoon I waxed eloquently on the benefits of handwriting in your journal, a few students pointed out that not everyone is comfortable writing by hand. Not everyone has a desk, and perhaps not all journaling needs to take place in a café.

If you cannot comfortably sit for ten minutes, what kinds of solutions can you invent?

Would a well angled tablet be more comfortable and welcoming? A lap desk? Tall counter? Tree fort? I encourage my clients and students to find a workable system that helps them create and journal rather than worry about the "right" way to do it. Remember this is just for you, there is no journaling contest, there is no journaling category at the county fair. There is no perfect writing position. Edith Wharton wrote in bed and tossed completed pages to the floor. (Where, I may add, an assistant retrieved them and typed them up, life was good for Wharton). A student found she was most comfortable writing while floating in the middle of her private pond. Which worked well in the summer. What is easier for you? Do that.

Because there are so many options, when you get stuck while working in one system, like typing on a keyboard, you can make the switch to handwriting, which can be both a relief and help inspire new ideas and better questions.

Journaling is a hobby blessedly free from comparison and competition.

I handwrite in an emergency, but for my daily journal, I prefer to type into an online program because my brain is much faster than my hand. There is a metaphor in that somewhere.

## 5
## WHAT KIND OF JOURNAL IS BEST?

The real question is what kind of journal will best suit your way of thinking and creating? But we don't want that answer, we want to know what is absolutely perfect. We ask a famous author what brand of pen she uses so we too can own that pen's magical qualities.

There is no single perfect journal, although there are enough options to stun you into a decision coma. Red? White? Glitter Trolls? Lined, unlined? On-line? Walk into a bookstore, you will quickly discover that journaling or at least the accouterments of journaling is a thing.

What to choose?

Pick a journal, chose an online or downloadable program and start, as you get better, more proficient and more proliferate, you'll change it up. Don't think change is defeat, I have many, many abandoned journals filled with inadequate ideas that I store for a brief time, then finally throw away. It's part of the creative process, part of the discovery process.

Since as a coach, I'm paid for certitude, here is the best journal.

. . .

## The Best Journal

The best journal is one that is not too fancy and not burdened with too many features. The best journal is easy to learn so you spend more time writing than you do finding ways to personalize your files. Even though there are beautiful, hard backed, end papered, glittered, gold leafed journals, you may want to start with a notebook that is not so intimidating. I have blank empty journals carefully stored on my shelf because I will never be able write sentences beautiful enough to justify the journal cover. The best journal can easily accommodate and contain bad words, crazy ideas and sloppy sentences.

I use Scrivener for my on-line journal and Rocket Books for notes. I use Mac Notes when I'm traveling with just my iPad, and I currently purchase notebooks by Lived-Inspired because the journals accommodate the typical sized postcard, and I still purchase postcards. As you journal, you will end up using more than one journal or notebook at any given time.

## This is your Creative Brain

After years of teaching, learning, researching then teaching again, here is what I know about creativity. It's not linear. Yet we live in a relentlessly linear world. Our stories move from point A to point B, our commute moves from home A to office B, our factories and food go from commodity A to product Q. Linear, easy to follow, measurable.

Completely unlike our brains.

Your brain often does not think, consider or contemplate anything in a nice linear fashion - a thought here, an idea there. Not to point fingers, but my own mind is very divergent which is a more complimentary term for random. I've learned to embrace my multiple interests and projects and created a journaling system to accommodate that.

If you start to write on one subject but then veer off to another subject, don't get discouraged, it's how we all think. Just allow that habitual ten-minute writing to unfold. Do not worry that the process or the unfolding ideas are not in line with a narrative or that you are not writing from A to B to C. No one does.

Journaling is the perfect way to capture and work on all the crazy ideas and seemingly random thoughts that float through your head. Remember you are channeling your subconscious, and your subconscious is not organized, that is a job for your journal. If the ideas have merit and are useful, then you wrestle them into a new document and only then inflict editing and peer review.

The best way to keep track of your ideas without squelching them is to keep multiple journals (perfectly reasonable), or tab sections in one large journal, or find an online journal that allows for different tabs and sections. For speed and organization, you can't beat working on a computer or tablet. It's easier to track and organize through computer-based journals. But as we discussed, if you are working on transformation, those hard copy journals are gold. You will probably want both.

### Possible journal categories

Free write journal - The messy one with all the cross outs and misspellings you can manage in the space of ten minutes.

Art journal - Paint, dream and paste stuff

Gratitude journal - Just how it sounds, this is a great separate section or journal just so it's easy to review when you need a lift.

Child or grandchild raising journal – Record what you

observe, make predictions that you are smart enough to keep to yourself. Date this journal just in case you need to tell your children that you knew all along this would happen.

Transition journal – Write about your transitions and keep track so you can return and admire your progress

Transformational journal – What do you want to happen? Did the writing help?

Affirmation – Gosh, Golly, I like myself! Or words to that effect. My own affirmation journal filled a single page. Which I threw away. You may have better luck.

Creative projects journal - Keep tabs on your creative life. Sketch out novel plots, develop characters, map out fabulous fantasy worlds. Keep these notes in one journal so you when you are ready to tackle your novel or story, all the notes are in one place.

Memoir – The one thing we can count on to move from A to Z is our life. Biography starts from the beginning and moves in a linear fashion to the end – yours or the biographers. Memoir is a moment, a week, a year of your life. If you are interested in writing a memoir, start making notes and saving them. Collect those ten-minute writes. After a year or so of notes, you may be ready to make sense of the whole thing. Don't edit this work until you are completely finished recording all those excellent evocative scenes and memories.

Family history – Record all those raucous and not quite accurate stories told every holiday. Corner an elderly family member and ask questions. Write it down. Your children won't give a damn, but your grandchildren will love you for it.

Poetry - Write poetry in a separate journal tab. No poem bursts forth in beautiful erudite phrases, more often they start as fragments, ideas and crappy unintelligible sentences, to be improved at a later date. Or never. Sometimes just capturing the thought of a poem is transformational enough.

My Scrivener journal has about 50 sections. Sections include projects, clients and a monthly journal space (so that's 12 sections right there). Blog ideas go into the blog section. Holiday gift ideas get filed into the holiday section.

You can do this with your on-line or electronic journal. You can do this with a series of small notebooks. You can do it with printed pages that are filed in big envelopes or folders.

I want you to freely write. There is no prescribed way to journal, except to do it. If you are writing for your own joy, that expression will manifest in your life in all sorts of ways. Try, do, journal.

**What about the Bullet Journal?**

The bullet journal is a great concept. Any system based on achieving your goals by systematically breaking down each goal to achievable steps is bound to be successful. In a bullet journal, those action steps are listed in each calendar day. Your only job is to check them off as they are accomplished.

Want to earn a million dollars by X date? Create a daily action plan filled with the steps that will bring you closer, closer, closer to that goal. Start investing into the IRA today, research a new position today, post your promotion on Linked-In today. Focusing on what you can do today is more manageable than creating, then facing the huge amorphous goal of Million.

There are hundreds of YouTube videos on the bullet journal, even more Pinterest boards dedicated to the practice. There is no dearth of information and how to feed and water your bullet journal.

The bullet journal is popular because ticking items off a list (any item off any list) is hugely satisfying. The catch is that any activity left on your Monday list needs to be copied to the Tuesday list. Didn't finish it on Tuesday? Write those remainders into Wednesday's list. You either get sick of repeatedly moving that item and just do it or you delete it for good. Either way, something happens.

## We Love Lists!

We will discuss lists later, but know even after that Bullet Journal rant, I am a big fan of making lists. I love checking off listed items so much I make lists of trivial, obvious activities:

1. Exercise
2. Breakfast
3. Shower

Just I can begin the morning with big checks next to three items.

Along with creating the daily important to do list, another list trend is to tackle our list in order of difficulty, placing the most difficult daily task first. Many business coaches including Steven Covey and Tim Ferris suggest taking on the biggest, baddest item on today's list first thing in the morning in order to get the damn thing over with. A popular term is "first eat the frog." Good advice since sometimes we spend more time worrying and fretting about a big, rather daunting task than if we just got the task over with. Finishing that onerous task early frees up the rest of the day for more enjoyable pursuits. No doubt about it. But.

Why are we eating frogs?

Before swallowing down frog legs, admittedly delicious with drawn butter, why do you need to eat this particular frog and why something so unappealing is on your list in the first place?

What I find interesting about the bullet journal and the whole craze around it, is the decided lack of narrative. Are we so task oriented, so busy, that we can't even lift our heads from our lists to consider why? No question our lives are full, before our first cup of coffee, our brain fires up like a gas-powered leaf blower, the to-dos cascade down threatening to overwhelm us.

### The leaf blower list

- Drive mother to the doctor.
- Create the copy for the non-profit newsletter
- Prepare the budget meeting
- Call parent to check in
- Call sibling because mother mentioned it
- Choose, sign and mail birthday cards
- Pick up after the dog
- Trim the grass (with a gas-powered weed-wacker).
- Dentist
- Take Tony to the airport
- Call about that funny ticking sound in the car
- Buy an outfit for the wedding
- Lose 35 pounds

### The frog list

- Write up the report
- Edit the report
- Fire Fred
- Hire Helen
- Schedule appt with CPA
- Approve the budget
- Hold a budget meeting anyway to discuss the approval
- Create a new mission statement
- Approve the ads that reflect the new mission statement
- Lose 35 pounds.

As they say, the list goes on and on. We tick off the budget meeting only to replace it with a strategy meeting. We call the parents only to make another note about another birthday we forgot and now need a mea culpa card to send ASAP.

We don't question the list. No one questions the list. We are not encouraged to evaluate the end game. We make the list to reach our million dollars yet fail to answer why having that specific amount of money is important.

We don't consider our own culpability in maintaining the list. We take a provided goal and dutifully make our monthly, weekly list to achieve that goal. We do all the tasks; we eat the frog. We are prisoners of our own efficiencies.

### Why are we eating frogs?

Let's question the list and every single item on it.

This may take more than a single journaling session. Maybe this is a week-long project.

Take an item or a related collection of items and write about them.

Journal about what you hate or love about each item. Do you hate the dentist appointment because it's painful or because the office music is terrible? Does the appointment take too long or is it because it's not covered by your insurance?

Do you shudder when you see cleaning on the to do list? Is cleaning and laundry always on the to do list because it's frigging endless?

What about that frog? What is so difficult that it needs to be quickly dispensed with? Does the "frog" represent just one small feature of your current work, or is it more than that?

These daily tasks take time, energy and often overwhelm

us to the extent that we end our days exhausted and unable to focus on what we really want or even focus on necessary action or change we desperately need to make to achieve better clarity, contribute to our community or advance our career in a meaningful way.

Write about not eating the frog at all. What if you dumped that frog onto another plate? What if you provided a bit of drawn butter to enhance the flavor?

What all this writing will eventually do is lead to a solution.

DELEGATION - HIRE OUT THE CLEANING, hire an assistant at work, send the frog over to Joe who just asked for more responsibility. Do not describe his new project as your frog.

**Gratitude** - Be grateful for the job, for the living parent, for the children.

**Time** - Nothing lasts forever even if it seems like forever at the time. Journal about what you will do with more time.

**Reality** - No matter what we do or how wonderfully transformed we are, we will still face crappy jobs and bad hair days. Life is not all glitter, rainbows and unicorns, because unicorns have very sharp horns and glitter never comes out of the carpet. Journaling about how you spend your days can be empowering. Do you approve your to do list? Have you created a day you won't regret tonight? That is something we can be pleased about since many of us like chicken more than frog.

## 6

## SET A TIME LIMIT

When we launch into a new project or set up a new healthy habit, our reaction is to immediately overdo. I love to overdo, it's one of my hobbies. And as expected, I almost always pay the price with burn out, perfection/rejection, bruises and finally giving up completely. Great response to a new project, right?

Don't pay the price. When we overdo, lifting 20-pound weights instead of five the first day at the gym, pushing our first morning jog into a run, extending our first ten-minute writing session into an hour . . . It's gives us an excuse to claim it is all too difficult if not impossible, so we need to quit. Forever. We tried, we whine, it was too hot to run, too stormy to drive to the gym, got a hand cramp.

Knowing this, that we often go big, then slink home empty handed, when we say journal for ten minutes, it's not a suggestion. Like building muscle, slow and steady will get you farther faster than one huge monstrous effort that will require two weeks of recovery.

A journaling time limit actually helps the subconscious be

more efficient. With only ten minutes scheduled to write, you must choose the most important issues and memories to write down. You need to focus and prioritize, staying with the energy, putting the other thoughts into their categories to review, but not to explore. Limited time is an effective frame to help you focus. It also keeps you from getting frustrated and even bored. We can do anything for ten minutes. Here is your chance to try.

WRITE for ten minutes without your editor or your conscious monkey-chattering-mind getting in the way. Write furiously and fully.

Write the truth.
Write until your fingers bleed.
How does that feel?
What did you discover?

### No Second Guessing

For transformative journaling to work, you need to write things as they come to you - clearly and with no judgement or rationalization. Just write it down, if you want, you can review later and slot the most interesting ideas into your various files and journals.

### IMAGES and weird stuff (like dreams)

What images come to mind when you focus on a situation? Record and describe the images as they appear in your mind's eye.

Don't interpret them, at least not right now.

Describe them, sketch them, hand write them, and then move on. When you return in a day or a week or a month, you'll be able to better appreciate the image, or at the very least, endow it with a useful label.

## No Editing!

Don't edit while you write.

In fact, one of the most beautiful features of your journal is you NEVER need to edit. Let your mind and imagination loose. Capture what you feel, what you want and how you'll get there. It has nothing to do with syntax or grammar unless you have made perfect grammar a dubious goal.

Consider writing in your journal for ten minutes time well spent and the first accomplishment of the day (yes, check it off your list). Reward yourself. If you want to write for longer than ten minutes tomorrow, set that as your intention and goal, but during these first few weeks, don't exceed your promised time.

7
---
# TIME

Ten minutes? TEN minutes? I hear you, in our busy lives, who has ten extra minutes to write? Yes, we are time crunched, the irony of faster cars is the traffic that slows us every morning to a crawling 10 miles/hour. The irony of instant entertainment is there is still nothing on. The irony of time saving devises is we just use them to get twice as much done so we can fall behind at an increasingly accelerate rate.

Let's spend a minute to see if we can find nine more in the day to start journaling.


**Crazy Busy**

Why are we so busy? I have read about it, considered it, and come to the conclusion that culturally, we love being busy. Over the last hundred years, busy has become emblematic of worth, a badge of honor. Who hasn't encountered a very sincere and frazzled young woman who brightly declares that she is crazy busy? And what more mature person finds it difficult to admit publicly that he spent the afternoon in the garden and forgot to check his phone? Your journal has no judgement. Write why you are so busy. You don't even need to address that maddening to do list and all those checked off frogs. Just write about busy.

What would you do if you weren't so busy?

Busy may be unavoidable. Back in the day, every morning was a tribute to very busy. Children needed to find socks to wear to school that was scheduled to start four minutes prior to the office opening. Traffic, lunches, parking. It was a frantic way to begin the day, and never seemed to ease up. But as we have seen, that can change. Through no fault of our own, the commute changes, the school hours change. We have just experienced an unexpected and heady time maybe we can embrace change as not only interesting, but an opportunity to take back our time. While our commutes and school systems catch up to the 21$^{st}$ century, here are some busy categories we can address now or as notes in your journal.

**Clutter**

We binged on Maria Kondo changing lives by cleaning clutter, so I don't need to belabor how physical clutter can be emotionally and physically detrimental. But in the interest of finding that additional ten minutes, consider how many minutes you spend searching for lost or misplaced things. It is easy to lose things in clutter: keys, wallet, phone. It can be easy to lose things even if there is not much clutter at all. Consider specific places for specific things and more importantly, get every family member to agree on that spot and follow through. If car keys always belong in the ceramic dish by the front door, you'll never need to hunt them down again. Which means you can re-claim those precious minutes to journal.

. . .

### New Project Busy

During the lock down, homemade sourdough bread became an Instagram trend. I found the trend entertaining because I lived through the Great Homemade Bread Movement of 1976. My father baked sourdough everything (the donuts were a bust) so I had some experience with the process. I also know that the more you bake and eat, the larger you get.

But sourdough rose to the top of my husband's list. A friend dropped off some starter and followed up with an instruction call. It was a long call. There were many steps, processes, and daily duties (put it on the to do list). Put this in, feed it with that, mix it. Buy better flour, buy better water. Do this every day (for ten minutes?) Don't forget. Not even once. As I helplessly listened to the elaborate instruction and lists of dos and don'ts I realized I was completely uninterested in sourdough starter. I can't even keep plants alive let alone an innocent culture of gas and potential. When the call was over, I admitted to my husband that this whole culture keeping, dough rising, bread baking seemed like too much work.

To my great relief, he agreed. We could walk to the bakery and buy exactly what we wanted. Ten minutes? I gained back hours of time even before squandering them on a project that I found far more stressful than relaxing.

That's the thing. You can say no. You can look at all the possibilities and interesting hobbies and required exercises and choose what you want to spend time on. And when you want to free up time for another different, satisfying project, trade. Give up the bread, gain the music. Give up the hand quilting, gain the home gym. Give up naming the birds in the back yard and just listen.

**The packed schedule**

We have many roles and it seems that every role requires

meetings or gatherings, and every meeting needs a homemade sourdough snack.

We all find great satisfaction in community efforts. We want to contribute to a project larger than we are. We want to give back. As members of society, taking part in public life is a good thing.

Until it's not.

How many hours do you volunteer? You can free up a week's worth of timed journal writing just by eliminating one organization meeting. But you can't give up that meeting because they are depending on you. You can't give up that other meeting because they just named you volunteer of the year. And of course, you cannot leave any group that voted you president.

There is a reason, *stop me before I volunteer again* is a popular meme.

If your volunteer work feeds your soul, if the groups to which you belong are populated by your people and you feel comfortable and comforted by the membership - stay. If your church is a joy - stay. Community is tremendously important and whether it's book club or temple, if the organization feeds your need for community and companionship, that group has earned your time.

But what if your calendar is packed with events, meetings, clean-up crews, snack schedules (gluten free, dairy free, sugar free, sourdough) and more time-vampire activities than you can manage?

Turn to your journal. Spend the next week writing about your clubs and service groups. List what you belong to and write a short essay or description of each one.

Now spend some time in review.

What do you like?

Why did you join? (Can you even remember why you joined?)

Do you love what you do?
Do you love their mission?
Is the group delivering reciprocal love and appreciation?
What have you contributed over the years?
What do you contribute now?
Is there role or job you want to discontinue?
Is there a club you want to discontinue?
Is there another role or job in the club that speaks to you?

The ancient Egyptians believed all thoughts originated from the heart because when you are sad, your heart aches. They weren't too far wrong. Journal about what makes your heart ache.

Now imagine and record what it would be like to NOT attend a certain set of meetings, or not chairing the next large community event. Journal about what you would lose, write about what you would gain.

- Are you worried about what others will think?
- Are you concerned that no one else will step up?
- Are you convinced that no one can do the same job as you?
- What if they did NOT do the same job as you?
- What if they do a BETTER job than you?

Address it all, the good, bad and ugly. Write a story about your day without this club or meeting. What else would you do? What else do you want to do?

I am a life-long volunteer, so it was no surprise I raised my hand and joined a newly forming Rotary Club. It seemed like a good idea at the time.

It was a good idea. Until it was not.

During my year as President, my journal pages exponentially increased. I lamented on paper so I wouldn't express my frustrations with the members. I struggled with my own personal satisfaction against the needs and demands of the club. It seemed I was working very hard and no one really cared. After many, many journal pages I realized that essentially, the members of this club simply were not my people. An obvious conclusion but getting there took a year of journaling plus a great many chicken lunches.

The journaling helped because I couldn't really talk with anyone in the club, and when I brought it up with friends, they just told me to quit. But as we just listed above, it's always more complicated than just "leave".

I began by sketching out the pros and cons in my journal to help with both clarity and courage. Then a dear friend who is just as prone to volunteerism as I, suggested a gradual exit involving missing a few meetings, then asking for a leave of absence for six months, then simply failing to return. That worked. It was a non-confrontational way to ease from the group.

About a year after I resigned, I was asked to speak to the club about my recent book. When the chicken lunch and my talk was finished, one of the members, a key player in my decision to leave the group, hugged me, and cheerfully suggested that I re-join the group because they missed me.

I smiled and graciously declined, which was another skill I was learning through journaling.

It's difficult to quit anything, and the perception of sunk costs can be overwhelming, with all this invested time, how can you possibly leave? Journaling can help plot out what you may gain. Once I wrestled back the four hours a week I formally devoted to the club, I could concentrate on projects that did feed my soul. I would not have escaped without journaling.

### Know your Role

What are your roles?

What are your public roles?

What are your titles both in the past and right now?

What do you always take on?

What do you always end up doing?

Do you like what you always end up doing? (I'm looking at you home baked snacks)

What do others assume about you because of your roles? (Is that good?)

Are you always the secretary?

Do club members automatically vote you president? (And did that happen during the only meeting you've ever missed?)

Do you want to be president?

What kind of crown do you want to wear?

Fluffy

Heavy

Festooned with jewels and prestige?

What kind of roles do you love and want to keep?

What makes your heart sing

WRITE down all that those feelings and ideas.

Is there a way of choosing one over the other?

Is there a way out?

Is there a way in?

How do you spend your time? If it's worth it, then keep the role, the title and the meetings. If you come to realize that the title isn't helping or advancing your own agenda and goals, and the time is becoming more vampire than volunteer, time to find a way out. I am rooting for you!

**Electronic clutter**

It takes 20 minutes or more to re-focus your attention after a distraction (I read that on an email that pinged into my feed.)

Every time we hear a ping, we react. We not only lose a

few minutes on the distraction, but we forfeit many more precious minutes mulling over the new information, processing it, then fighting our way back to the task at hand. Just when we hit the creative zone again, ping! It could be another friend in Tanzania who lost her wallet, or it could be an agent responding to our book query of seven months ago. Already distracted, we open another email, then another, ooh, I may have already won!

Reacting itself is addicting. Reacting is busy. We look busy, we feel busy. We respond to email and notifications while listening in on a conference call and editing an article due in an hour. Our Puritan ancestors would be thrilled with our ability to do it all – all at once. Knit while you pray, talk while you plant, read the bible during those long cart rides to the next village. Theirs and our philosophy is essentially multitaskers can't get in trouble. Very busy people are too unfocused and distracted to do any harm. You light multiple fires in the morning so you can spend the afternoon stamping them to ash.

How does journaling help manage all this screen clutter?

Isn't writing down even more words just adding to the problem?

Not really.

By spending ten minutes to half hour a day focusing on your journaling you have, for that time, ignored all the pinging, hopping and reacting and just focused on the task at hand, writing.

It's like working out one muscle group at a time. The more you do it, the stronger the muscle. The stronger your muscles, the better you feel.

Writing is like that too: the more you do, the better you get, the stronger you feel.

**Before and after**

Write for ten minutes with no interruptions. Don't scan

the mail. Don't pick up the phone (this is why first thing in the morning is so helpful, fewer notifications). How do you feel after writing nonstop? How do you feel after focusing on a project exclusively for ten, twenty or thirty minutes?

Repeat the writing exercise the next morning, but this time, allow your attention to wander. Open the emails, check for texts, skim through twitter. Check the weather app.

How much writing did you do?

More importantly, how does trying to just write for ten minutes feel in the face of extreme distraction?

Lock the experience of working distraction free in your brain and body. Practice with other projects. See what happens.

By the way, this whole conversation about excess stuff can be understood generationally. Younger people often drown in spontaneous purchases while the older generation drowns in uncomfortable and ugly inherited stuff. Most of the resistance to clearing out our stuff is based on the theory of sunk cost - we spent this money, so we need to keep it, our grandparents brought this from the old country, so we need to keep it.

We all have our stories. What journaling can do is illuminate and record the stories. The stories are what matter in the first place, so write them down. Journaling about your stuff can be the starting point for actually moving those things to a better use, or a better place.

Take a photo of the ugly uncomfortable couch and write up its story. Once you get the whole story out, it will be easier to move that particular item out of your house to a better home, at least that's what I told my mother.

# 8
# MIND MAPS AND TIMELINES

Mind Maps are organization charts gone rouge. They are both appealing and appalling – all those wobbly circles and heavy lined squares linked by thick or dotted lines connecting them (on a good day) and creating a visual representation of a flawlessly interconnected company or project or event.

You can create your own interconnected, organized, crazy chart complete with circles, boxes and questionable connections. What a mind map can do is put a question or idea into a different visual form so it's easier to see.

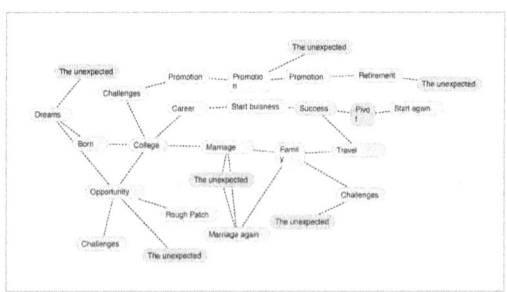

8

## MIND MAPS AND TIMELINES

Mind Maps are organization charts gone rouge. They are both appealing and appalling – all those wobbly circles and heavy lined squares linked by thick or dotted lines connecting them (on a good day) and creating a visual representation of a flawlessly interconnected company or project or event.

You can create your own interconnected, organized, crazy chart complete with circles, boxes and questionable connections. What a mind map can do is put a question or idea into a different visual form so it's easier to see.

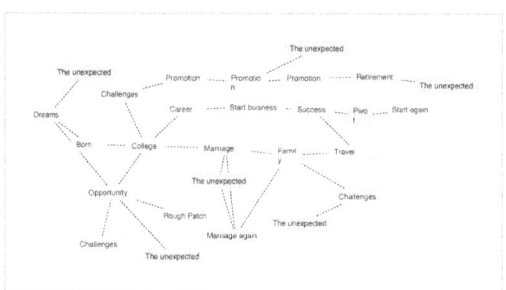

the mail. Don't pick up the phone (this is why first thing in the morning is so helpful, fewer notifications). How do you feel after writing nonstop? How do you feel after focusing on a project exclusively for ten, twenty or thirty minutes?

Repeat the writing exercise the next morning, but this time, allow your attention to wander. Open the emails, check for texts, skim through twitter. Check the weather app.

How much writing did you do?

More importantly, how does trying to just write for ten minutes feel in the face of extreme distraction?

Lock the experience of working distraction free in your brain and body. Practice with other projects. See what happens.

By the way, this whole conversation about excess stuff can be understood generationally. Younger people often drown in spontaneous purchases while the older generation drowns in uncomfortable and ugly inherited stuff. Most of the resistance to clearing out our stuff is based on the theory of sunk cost - we spent this money, so we need to keep it, our grandparents brought this from the old country, so we need to keep it.

We all have our stories. What journaling can do is illuminate and record the stories. The stories are what matter in the first place, so write them down. Journaling about your stuff can be the starting point for actually moving those things to a better use, or a better place.

Take a photo of the ugly uncomfortable couch and write up its story. Once you get the whole story out, it will be easier to move that particular item out of your house to a better home, at least that's what I told my mother.

### Mind Maps

Mapping allows for a different kind of thinking - it gives us space to consider new and former ideas as well as being able to see how those boxes and circles have served or hindered over the years.

### Timelines

Timelines, like mind maps can give you a break from writing as well as help you create a strong visual of where you are and where you may be heading.

Both timelines and maps are by nature, linear to begin with, but as you work them, and fill them in, you'll discover detours, roads not taken, ideas undeveloped. Allow for all that, this is a great exercise to show you where you've been as well as highlight all the roads yet to be traveled.

What many of my students discovered was that once they created the basic timeline, they were absolutely compelled to add in more details as well as historical commentary and revisionist editorials. This is all good.

Create your timeline and mind maps based on your history, your journey and your creative life.

#### TIMELINE SUBJECTS

- Your relationships
- Your career path
- Your educational path
- Your emotional path
- Choices you've made
- Your creative life
- Your successes both creatively and personally

Are there obvious or subtle patterns in the mapping?
What do you see?
While we are still deep into the map metaphor, write about one of the circles or squares on your map.
The square labeled college -

- What were you thinking?
- Who gave you good directions?
- Teacher
- Relative
- Spouse
- Friends
- Parents

Who gave you terrible directions?

- Bad (exciting) lover
- Bad (exciting) uncle
- Well-meaning grandparent
- Professors

(You can see that this resembles the Hasbro *Game of Life*)

- What unnecessary detours did you take?
- What drove you off the road
- What do you think their motivation was?
- Even if the directions were pretty good, would you follow them today?

**How is your driving?**
When you review the road map what do you notice about your own course?

- When faced with a road sign, do you always turn left?
- What if you turned right?
- Do you drive slow or fast?
- Do you eschew tourist traps?
- Do you stop at every historical marker? (Looking at you, dad).
- Do you avoid travel all together?
- What would happen if you just kept driving east?

This exercise is not meant to create a morass of grief and regrets. And it's not meant to encourage you to wallow in the past. An exercise like this can point to your "shoulds", your internal obligations. If you can identify those obligations, imposed internally or (often) imposed externally, and if you can sketch them out and review them, maybe you can change how you regard them, maybe even move past them.

Maybe explore an altogether different road.

# JOURNAL FOR BETTER FAMILY RELATIONSHIPS

If you have the perfect family, you can skip this chapter with my blessings and disbelief.

"Happy families are all alike; every unhappy family is unhappy in its own way." Family members can be challenging, it's their job. One of the best defenses against a loving, sharing, caring family is your journal. Journaling can help you step away from some of the self-referential drama and practice how to be amused instead of aggravated.

You know that changing other people is difficult to impossible. What journaling can bring is an opportunity for you to change how you react to the family. Change your own responses and actions and that change alone will help make family life if not perfect, than at least easier. What if the next holiday was stress free? How can you achieve that? Journal about it.

Again, I'm not a therapist, probably because like right now, instead of allowing you to spend time and materials to find your own solutions, I just tell you what to do (apparently that's a therapy don't). I do know that your journal can be the vehicle that will transform the dysfunctional present to the practically perfect fully functional future. Just by focusing and writing down what you really want.

To transform your responses and thus a family member's reactions, you will need to journal with intention.

Can you break down the problem?

"My mother never approved of my husband" Can you drill that down to even more specific examples? How do you know she disapproves? What does she say? Does she withhold affection? Sniff at his attempts at conversation? Make snide comments? Write furiously in her journal every morning? Write out the triggers.

Write out the ideal familial exchange. Practice it next time you walk into the family drama, remembering that you hold the only revised script.

Recording our feelings and desired outcomes is critical. What do you want to happen? Do you want the kids to move out? Do you want your mom to accept your new partner? Do you need support for your new business venture? Do you want to stop attending a particularly difficult family holiday meal or annual reunion?

Just noticing and writing down what is happening and what you'd rather see and experience will get you 95% of the way there. The next step is write down what YOU will do during the next family get together. Own your own reactions. Maybe you write down how you plan to smile and hug cousins, aunts and uncles and ignore their small repetitive comments. Maybe you express deep pleasure when Mom or Dad offer up a compliment (positive reinforcement). Or you write out a scenario during which you walk away from your (still) annoying brother as he grows increasingly drunk.

Your job is to write what happens, write what you want to happen, what you will do to make that happen, then practice the new script and responses during the next family reunion.

It may take a few weeks or even months to follow through

*The Journal Book*

on this particular change so don't try to change everything and your responses to everyone all in the same evening. Choose a single reaction to encourage. Write about what it looks like, what you look like, and what the ideal reaction will be. Then try it.

Remember to write about the results but focus on you. How did that feel for you to respond differently? Congratulate yourself on your new behavior and being pro-active instead of reactive.

That inaugural success can engender even more successes and even further positive behavior. You may end up so happy you won't know what to do with yourself.

## 9
## TALK TO THE DEAD

Journaling is faster and more effective
than consulting a Ouija board

In the mid 19th century, not un-coincidentally right after the Civil War, spiritualism once again rose up and consumed the middle class.

Contacting the dead was as popular a pastime as checking in on Facebook. The way it worked was you, the bereaved widow, contracted with a self-selected medium who promised to reveal where your late husband hid all the gold he bragged about when alive. The medium used many methods of communication, table knocking, channeled voices, dramatic re-enactments, all for a price. In a later twist, some spiritualists channeled the dead through what they called automatic writing. The channeler would simply take dictation from the spirit world so loved ones could read for themselves the very words of their dearly departed.

We can only imagine how disappointing it was to not get a scrawled version of a map to the buried gold.

Even if the effort was fake, the spiritualists were on to

something. While knocking on tables and claiming the apparition hovering over your head was uncle Theo back from the war was quickly debunked, automatic writing stuck. But instead of channeling ghosts, the writer is channeling the subconscious.

You can return to that idea to talk to the dead.

Most of us in the US are singularly bad at death. When a loved one passes, there is actually a socially sanctioned option to ignore the whole messy business. The bereaved can pretend they are not bereaved at all. Everything is fine, nothing has changed, move on. But unsurprisingly ignoring emotional trauma leads to more stress than you deserve. Stress, particularly the one-sided stress associated with loss, can create a maelstrom of symptoms and health challenges.

In my family, D' Nile is not just a river. Most members of my family resisted grieving or even acknowledging the deaths of their loved ones. I assume they were loved ones.

I've witnessed first-hand the physical manifestations of not dealing directly with emotional loss. After my grandfather died of a heart attack, my grandmother did not cry, mourn, throw ashes on her head, cut her hair or even call the family for a wake. Everything was fine. Move on. Nothing to see here.

She absolutely denied that the subsequent three months of:

- Shingles
- Returning cancer
- Emotional instability
- Early death

Was all a coincidence.

If you don't acknowledge grief, your body will do it for you.

If you don't want to choose that option, use your journal as your mental health tool and a safe place to vent grief, rage, acceptance, bargaining all those normal emotions when working through a loss. Get it all out. If you have to deal, if you must solider on, your journal will be the best place to vent, and keep you healthy and sane.

Even if you don't trigger cancer, I found another frightening list of the possible outcomes of un-acknowledged grief:

- Becoming easily agitated, frustrated, and moody
- Feeling overwhelmed, like you are losing control or need to take control
- Having difficulty relaxing and quieting your mind
- Feeling bad about yourself (low self-esteem), lonely, worthless, and depressed
- Loss of Sexual Desire and/or ability
- Clenched Jaw, teeth grinding
- Forgetfulness
- Inability to focus
- Pessimism

I'm a fan of reaching out to friends, whiskey, large Irish wakes and therapy, maybe all at once. But even those outlets, plus stylish black outfits, are often not enough. Journal. I particularly appreciate journaling to talk to the dead when I wasn't close to the deceased but still need closure. Maybe it takes more than a party and a journal entry to find closure and start healing. Humans need ceremony, monuments, Ancestor Days, Day of the Dead. If those ceremonies are unavailable, for our health, we may need to create our own ceremonies and acknowledgments.

## Speak Up

Journal out dialogues, conversations and what you always meant to say to the deceased. No, it won't do THEM any good, this is about you.

When you pull out your journal to talk to your dead, what do you say?

Finish up unfinished business. Often this approach, finishing what was left on the table, leads to very interesting memoirs and histories.

Write out a dialogue with your loved (or not so loved) one

- I feel bad you left
- You left too soon
- You finally left, and now it's too late
- Appreciate them
- Yell at them
- Forgive them

Write about what you will do now. What have you been waiting to do? You can be as honest as you want, no one will read your journal. It's just for you, it's your recovery.

A student actually carried on an excellent conversation with her recently deceased father. She was searching for a particular document hidden in his messy unorganized files and was at the end of her patience. She wrote out a long letter to her father in her journal and asked for his help. She slept on it.

The next morning, she returned to that very same box of letters, notes and certificates and pulled out the exact document she had been searching for. She was pleased not only to find the document, but that Dad finally came through.

Talking to the dead often will not be confirmed to a single

ten-minute exercise. It may take months or even a year to work through a recent death, and we don't know, as we practice our version of automatic writing, what else will appear. But the more we get out on paper, the more we write, the better we feel.

## 10
## WHAT'S YOUR STORY?

One of the perks of traveling across an enormous ocean in a smelly, leaky boat heading to a new world you knew nothing about before reading the flyer advertising the bargain passage was the ability to invent your own story once you arrived. In the US, reinvention is a tradition. In California, it's an art.

The new world demanded stories. If you, the third child of the fourth in line for whatever property was left after the Restoration, traveled for long tedious months in the hold of a cramped ship to reach the shores of what promised to be a great new place and opportunity (because you believed the ad), and what you found fell considerably short of expectations, how to describe the experience to the family waiting to hear from you back in the old country?

You invent. You write out a new story. And in the American tradition of storytelling, you also exaggerate. Yup, you wrote home, the streets ARE paved with gold, I'm picking up the nuggets as we speak. Crazy busy, will write more later.

Some stories ended up published and read. Some were

just a way to get through the day since the purported gold lined streets were in fact covered in excrement and garbage.

You had to make up a new story, it was the only way to survive.

## Your Story

Your story is important, it defines not only who you are but also who you want to be as well as signal how you want to interact with the world. Your story can of course, be all about your past, but when we become conscious about our own story, it often becomes rooted in what we want in the future. The idea of a self-made person, the person you want, not the person you were yesterday. Your story is written and performed by you alone.

During a happy hour mixer for creatives, introductions did not revolve around what do you do, or even who is your family, or where do you live, all markers for economic and social status, the question was what are you doing, what are you inventing, what is your art?

Discussing our art gave us permission to create better, more interesting stories about ourselves. A story around invention and art is a story that will carry you farther than a clunky sentence about accounting practices.

And if you have a passion project, if you are exploring your new art, or a new idea, this is the ideal conversational lead.

## What if it's the wrong story?

I work with business clients who not only cannot describe or express their essential mission, they can't even land on their story, not even as a party trick. Some abdicate the responsibility and appoint a committee to create the company story. This is how lengthy values statements are made, each sentence representing the agenda of every individual committee member in the room: wasted time and energy.

You cannot attract what you want in your business or life if your story doesn't work.

A GOOD STORY is bold and daring. A real story is exciting, something you never tire of hearing or telling. We expect bold and daring stories from start-ups and indie bands, not from regular companies or average lives. But those lives count. Those stories are important. Don't let the story of your business languish or be ignored, revisit it, write it with excitement and wonder in mind.

Another challenge for clients is how to describe the story of their book (or artistic project). The problem starts with their insistence that their book (or product) is for everyone. The project will be wildly popular, the story is universal.

Imagine Frankenstein's monster created by committee: each person contributing their ideal arm, their personal vision of a leg, a foot provided by their brother's new factory. The creature would have all the parts, maybe stand, but it is impossible for the poor thing to coordinate all those disparate parts well enough to move forward.

You want to move forward.

### How to create your story

How can you write up a good personal story?

Connect your heart back to your head. It may take a few tries and a couple hours writing in your journal to get there, but worth the exercise.

- What do you really want?
- How do you want to introduce yourself?
- What is your ubiquitous thirty second elevator speech? (When we can once again join people in elevators.)
- What should your bio, that short introduction before the full detailed story, say about you and where you want to go?
- What are you proud of?
- Why do you live here and not there?
- How did your family or background help you?
- How did your family hinder you and why do you need to write up a different origin story?
- How do you express your authentic self?

RECORD YOUR OWN TRUTH, describe your unique experiences and viewpoint. Ironically, the more specific and honest you are, the more appealing your story will be to others.

Our stories are interesting when they reveal the essence of who we are and what we really want in the world. Those specific, detail rich stories are compelling and driving, and when you are clear, armed with a good story – you will find just the right audience ready to listen.

## 11

## YOUR PASSION PROJECT

Your journal can reveal unremembered passions, interests and ideas. Reviving former passions can lead to new projects, an innovative business, a new absorbing hobby or a second career. Your journal will reveal what you need and if you're lucky, how to do it, what steps to take. The goal is to find a project that gives back. Become involved in a passion project, and surprisingly, the rest of your life will noticeably improve. My goal is to encourage you to find more in life than just checking off obligations from a to do list.

### Dad's Passion Project

My father loved teaching high school, and he was good at it, or he was at least memorable. Rather than teach to the bitter end, he took early retirement in order to take on his passion project, his second career.

I will never forget my dad's reaction when asked what he did. "I was a high school teacher," he'd mutter, but then he raised his head, his eyes lit up, and he'd yell, "but LET ME

TELL YOU about what I'M DOING NOW." His passion project, producing and touring travel films, gave him ten years of utter pleasure.

When asked the inevitable question, what do you do, we tend to search for an answer within very narrow boundaries so often the only activity that comes to mind is our job. The only thing worth discussing is what we do to in order to pay the bills. Don't describe what you do, explain who you are.

Life is not about the career or the job, it's about what you love.

Passion Projects are messy, peripatetic, and priceless. Passion Projects are hobbies gone walkabout dragging you along for the journey. When describing a Passion Project, my clients usually begins with — it's always something I wanted to do. Like my father, their whole face lights up when they describe their crazy, deeply involving project.

A Passion Project is not a bucket list. You aren't ticking off items from yet another, albeit, long standing list. Pluck one of those bucket list items and go deep. Buy and read the books, collect memorabilia, start a blog, attend the lectures, participate in conferences, take classes, join groups, travel to the sites, visit the museums. Passion and focus will inform every next step. Passion Projects exist and are pursued for no other purpose than enrichment, no other reason than living more deeply with greater concentration and focus. A good passion project will keep you in the zone all day.

Passion Projects do not belong to someone else. You are not in a passion project if you are helping or driving or suffering in silence as your partner marks off every move on the battlefield at Gettysburg (or, in the case of my husband, required to travel to Sussex to visit Virginia Woolf's home. I love him so much I left him at home while I took that pilgrimage with my niece).

Passion projects can be the deep study of a single

subject or person. This can lead to wine tasting trips to Provence, walks to St. James, castle tours in Germany. It can lead to taking classes and later teaching classes. The Osher Lifelong Learning programs are predicated on passion projects. Who better to teach a class than someone who is so fascinated about a subject, done all the work and now want to share?

Best feature of a passion project? They don't produce income. None of the above pursuits makes money. Not a single hour of practice and study translates into cash. Which is much the point.

A Passion Project is the answer when asked, what do you do? I am studying El Greco and am interested in the political subtext in his more famous paintings. I've just scheduled a trip to Spain to further research the works themselves.

I am learning the ukulele and am now playing in a group and we are all traveling to The Big Island to refine our strumming.

It sounds indulgent and, in some contexts, it can be. But it's also empowering and enlightening. If you are pursuing your passion, if what you are doing really wakes you up, then other ideas and opportunities will present themselves, related to your project or not. That's what I want for you.


### How to forge a new more creative path

Re-connect with what you've always wanted to do.

Look at your road map, was there a detour you've always wanted to take? A missed opportunity? Double back and see where that may lead.

- Discover old artistic impulses and act on them.
- What you don't need is another academic degree.
- What you don't need is outside validation.

- What you don't need is to immediately monetize the effort.
- Buy cheap paints and start painting.
- Dig up a half-used school journal and write for ten minutes a day.

Take local classes, take seminars, join workshops, join meet ups - focus on improving your work for you, not for sale, not for a juried show, but for you.

Experiment with what art pulls you into a zone you haven't experienced since you were five years old.

Do that.

## 12

# JOURNAL FOR CREATIVE MOJO

Journaling is a great help in facilitating the creative process. Here are a few journaling methods that will get you from mired to inspired.

### You have run out of ideas

Journal about how you've run out of good ideas.

Write for ten minutes in your journal about everything you really want to say on target subject, any subject. This is particularly helpful if you are still working on discovering your passion project. It may take more than just a ten-minute write, but if you keep at it, day by day, interesting work will start to rise to the top or at least hide in the middle of a paragraph.

Record whatever comes to mind, possible novel scenes, dialogue, ideas for photography, sculpture, a new trip. With consistency, random thoughts will either flare up and disintegrate into ash or actually catch fire.

· · ·

## You waste too much time thinking

Write it out. We often ruminate so hard and so long on a difficult section of our creative work in progress that it feels as if we actually did the work. Thinking can leave us more exhausted than simply doing the work.

Stop worrying and write. Journal about your creative angst in general as well as the specific block in particular.

Review your writing. Is there a theme? Is there a discoverable block or problem that can be more specifically addressed? Take that observation and journal about *that* for a few days. Allow for the tedious repetition of this exercise because the benefit of this work is you will get bored with your own circular thoughts and start to search for a solution.


## You are uninspired

Make an appointment for inspiration.

Jack London advised hunting down inspiration with a club. You can certainly do that but showing up is another equally and less violent way to court the Muse.

Show up every morning ready to write whatever comes to mind. Do this consistently enough and soon the Muse will stop by and join you for coffee. Keep the appointment and she will appear to help.

### The journaling itself is getting dull

Move. If you usually journal on a laptop in a local cafe, journal on your bed using a pen and a legal pad.

If you write every morning long hand in a leather-bound book in your Downton Abbey library, journal on a typewriter in a basement lit with a single lightbulb.

If you usually type out your work on your phone, journal using a stick in the sand.

In other words, mix up the whole thing for a different

perspective and a different way of writing, either slower or faster, either by hand or by key.

Once you find a different way to express yourself, the expression itself will be different. Set that into your work.

## 13

# THE PAIN AND PERILS OF STARTING OVER

Who hasn't had nightmares of losing their work? A friend reported that due to a bug (we hope it's not a feature), the most recent sixteen hours investment on his symphony had disappeared with no hope of recovery. Clients have watched in horror as novels are swallowed whole. I once lost a just completed workbook into the black maw of cyberspace where no one hears you scream.

What do you do when you've lost weeks, months, years of work?

First - scream anyway, cry and bang your head on the offending laptop.

Next - scream and beat the offending laptop against the floor.

Call a friend, then scream that they just don't understand.

Because after patiently listening to your rant, they sensibly asked why don't you just start over?

After a couple of gin and tonics, you wake to the painful realization that the only course of action is to actually start over, which you may have heard from someone yesterday, but you are pretty sure it's your own idea. And the third G & T was not a good idea, not even at the time.

You don't have to like it but starting a project over does have creative benefits.


### Time

For Creatives, time is our friend. Even a few days of distance helps us refine our work. Returning to the project after a few days away, or in this scenario, return to the project because you must, carries the benefit of maturity, even if you are merely a few hours older.


### THE MORNING After

Time can heal some wounds. If lucky, you return to a lost or abandon project and find the PPT template you thought lost. Or you discover the exact right musical beat that days prior, had eluded you. Or a new voice in your novel emerges from an unlikely, previously marginalized character.

**New energy for an old project**

You may review your just found work with a different perspective or attitude. Since you and your work survived the ultimate disaster, it may be easier to view the remains with a more critical eye. The next iteration is almost always stronger, better and able to leap tall agents and towering readers in a single bound.


### Fake Loss

Can we generate the energy and maturity of loss without all the angst, teeth gnashing and potential alienation of friends?

While we artists don't purposefully lose our work, we do

tend to abandon it for long periods of time. That abandonment has a purpose. It allows us to return to our work with fresh eyes and consider if it's worth continued investment. Can this be saved? Can this be edited? Or should we just shove it back into a dark file and move on?

Recent research on creativity validates this tendency to start a project well ahead of deadline, leave it for up to months at a time, then right before deadline, modify, edit and in some cases, rewrite the work, then turn it in. A deadline focuses our thinking and pulls out better ideas, more interesting turns of phrases. It can be good. It's often good.

Even if you don't have a deadline for your work, you can create one. Pick a time and day you want the project finished and create the work under the shadow of that looming date. Invest the deadline with gravitas and urgency. If you've convinced yourself that you must do this now, under this deadline, your focus will become sharp and clear.

And what about the time off between starting and (at last) finishing a project? It is time well spent offering up ideas, new materials, and rest.

The Muse is ready to help, you just need to give her the opportunity. What I have found is that while hanging out in the resting stage of a project, often the exact material I need pops up on my newsfeed. Or a conversation triggers a new way to look at the novel. Or a client calls and offers up a better story for my book.

If this is how your Muse works, how your process progresses, your best strategy is to allow it to happen. Don't erase or lose your first draft but do find a way to give it some breathing room. Is there a new project you can work on while the current one rests for a couple weeks? Can you take a vacation between the novel's first and second draft? Can you take up another art form and practice that for a week or two?

Or do you prefer to bang your head on the laptop and spend the trip money on a new computer?

Don't do something, just stand there.

## 14

## MAKING MISTAKES, AND WHY WE SHOULD

I teach a journaling class (you may know this). After my very first class the students requested a workbook based on the PowerPoint slides and lecture notes. I had about 24 hours to create the book before the class finished. They also requested continued meet-ups for more journaling practice. I did that too.

At the first meet up, Donna, one of the students arrived at the meet-up, sat down and announced she found typos in the handout.

She was very pleased to be the first to announce my mistakes.

"It is not the critic who counts; not the man who points out how the strong man stumbles, or where the doer of deeds could have done them better."

Our lives are overrun with critics. For many artists, criticism is kryptonite. Critics are confident where writers are timid. They are certain where painters have doubts. Critics can be so terrifying that many artists will simply stop making anything just to avoid censor and negative comments. We will work over an essay or a painting until holes are worn in the canvas and book chapters lose all color and light because we are so afraid of the critic, of making a mistake. We have no defense when faced with the self-righteous critic.

I thanked Donna and asked her to send the list of my mistakes so I could correct them.

She replied airily, "Oh there were just too many to count, I couldn't possibly make a list." She had no intention of helping, of moving a project forward. Her goal was to make sure that in this meeting, in this exchange, she was right, and I was wrong.

Surprisingly, I was neither crushed nor demoralized. I have learned that "credit belongs to the man who is actually in the arena, whose face is marred by dust and sweat and blood. . ."

Gladiators are different from spectators. Those of us who fight in the arena covered in dust, sweat and blood are actually quite kind to our fellow combatants. We offer help and a leg up, perhaps even over the stadium wall. Knowing what it is like to create, real creatives are far less likely to criticize without first offering to help. And if you tend to be critical just to be right, here is your chance to change.

- Do you want to criticize, or dare greatly?
- Do you want to find fault or discover marvelous alternatives?
- Do you want to demoralize or inspire?

When you launch into the world committed to your passion, you are daring greatly. You are doing, not watching. You are starting something that no one else has ever dared begin let alone nurture through to the end.

I have written twenty books none of which made the best seller list, a couple of which have earned enough money for a flat white grande. A critic would typically respond that only a book reaching best seller status is valuable, an easy assertion if you are not an author.

What matters to me is that I fulfilled the idea, completed the book and published because I want to share. Making books is what I do and who I am. The work is always glorious and life changing. I always emerge from the arena a different person, a better person, or at least a more knowledgeable person.

### Who is the Critic?

Some readers are helpful and give me a list of mistakes and their corrections. Others dismiss the whole effort because they found mistakes. (My mother read my recent book and found five typos. She did not mark them.) If this is the kind of feedback you get, do consider the source. Is the critic a fellow solider, a professional in your field? Has your critic done what you've done? Has he or she written a book? Submitted poems? Daily bled onto the page?

Because if not, well. . . .

### You Win

If you are a writer and a creator, you have already won the battle if not the war. Your daring, your effort guarantees that your " place shall never be with those cold and timid souls who neither know victory nor defeat."

Maybe poor Donna had never created. She never wrote, perhaps despite my class, she never started her journal. When a person is busy finding mistakes of others, they don't have time to make their own. That is a terribly cold place to live.

## 15

## THE MAN IN THE ARENA

EXCERPT FROM THE SPEECH "CITIZENSHIP IN A REPUBLIC" - 1910

It is not the critic who counts; not the man who points out how the strong man stumbles, or where the doer of deeds could have done them better. The credit belongs to the man who is actually in the arena, whose face is marred by dust and sweat and blood; who strives valiantly; who errs, who comes short again and again, because there is no effort without error and shortcoming; but who does actually strive to do the deeds; who knows great enthusiasms, the great devotions; who spends himself in a worthy cause; who at the best knows in the end the triumph of high achievement, and who at the worst, if he fails, at least fails while daring greatly, so that his place shall never be with those cold and timid souls who neither know victory nor defeat.

Theodore Roosevelt -
http://www.theodore-roosevelt.com/trsorbonnespeech.html

## 16

## PUSHING OVER THE STACK OF CREATIVE BLOCKS

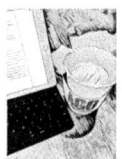

I believe in creative blocks, writer's block. I also believe that frustration, boredom and general despair is part of the creative life. It's not pretty, but if you understand that frustration is part of the creative process, it's easier to get through and you embrace these moments as leading indicators that you are standing at the edge of your breakthrough.

Sometimes we get so blocked that we start to question our entire creative endeavor. We start to research alternative activities, any activity besides writing, painting, music: water skiing, macrame, skydiving. Because what is the point? The point is to express your gifts, and spend as much time in the creative zone as possible because that zone is the happiest place a person can play in. But what if the playground is deserted?

### Nap Time

Our playground may be empty to give us a break. Every once in a while, the Muse must drag us from the park for a nap. We whine that we don't need to nap. Yes, replies the Muse, you do.

An important part of the creative process is thinking. Which unfortunately, looks like doing nothing.

Part of your process may be to allow the flow of life to carry you along for a while and land you on a shore made of better ideas and fresh material.

After our nap, we can put our wonderful obsession into perspective, if that is not a contradiction in terms. You have the opportunity to step back and understand - I'm not a failure because I didn't achieve this singular goal, I'm incubating an idea that will become large, fabulous and creative. And maybe it will take a little more than a month to manifest. Maybe a year. Maybe twenty.

Consider, then embrace, the idea that your creativity is expressed continually and in very different forms, that frankly, should be better honored. Embrace that there are other life projects that sometimes take center stage in your head and your heart. And when the guests depart, when the plane touches down, when the party is over, when the move is complete, when the paint dries in the last remodeled room, suddenly there will be space in your head to return to work.

From too many choices to not enough, our creative blocks are real. The best way to break through your blocks is to demolish them one block at a time. This is how.

**It seems counterintuitive but write down your blocks.**

Write for ten minutes on "I don't want to work on my creative project because . . ."

Don't get blocked recording your blocks! What else is bugging you?

What are you afraid of? Hangnails and bad hair count.

Also consider choice, do you have too many? It is easy to make a quick decision if the choice is limited between chocolate or vanilla, but all 39 flavors? Suddenly we are stumped. Can that be one of your creative challenges?

What if this project is a big success? Record all the positive outcomes.

What are the possible negative outcomes? Will the family disapprove? Will success actually cut into your artistic work?

Make an emergency creative list. Where can you go to get a big hit of, well, big?

Make an emergency list of house or yard cleaning projects that while morally laudable, are boring. Journal that since you can't come up with anything interesting for your book or essay, you may as well scrub the moss from the patio.

Sure enough, the next day an absolutely divine solution for your work will appear and you'll need to spend the whole morning creating while the patio remains covered in fuzzy green stuff. There is power in faking yourself out.

# TECH

**Of all the writing advice, the most difficult to do, the scariest thing to try is leave the phone behind.**

At this point in your journaling and creative journey, you know:

- To show up every day to write, at roughly the same time, so your Muse can find you just as suggested in the *Artist's Way*.
- To honor your writing as work and protect that time, just like Natalie Goldberg tells us to do in *Writing Down the Bones*.
- To leave behind negative people and situations that are hindering or even killing your creativity just like in *How To Journal*.
- To enhance your own writing by taking up an alternative hobby, if you write, play music. If you play music, dance. If you dance, keep a journal.
- To always learn. To that end, you have registered

for a community college extension class in the Art and Uses of Greek Pottery.
- To break down your goals into manageable chunks of time and effort, just like in Anne Lamont's *Bird by Bird*.
- To keep a journal.
- To study something deeply.
- To read deeply.
- To sleep.
- To turn off your phone

I can hear you from here. Turn off the phone? What if someone needs me? What if there is news? What if I need to post a photo of this rock? What if I need to post a selfie on the beach so my friends know what I'm up to? What if they post something I don't want to miss: a puppy, a kitten, a politician on fire. It's important to know everything all at once, all right now. As if knowing equals action, as if knowing equals peace.

**The Phone Free Morning**

Sunday morning my husband and I climbed into his truck and bounced down a long narrow potholed dirt road to Purdon's Crossing, on the Yuba River. We hiked down to the water's edge and spent the morning sitting on the hot rocks, swimming in the cool water, admiring the green pines against the blue sky, listening to the water rush around the rocks while a dog with a horrible high yipping bark, swam and barked for an hour and a half.

We parked at a drive-in and ate lunch outside on a picnic bench. With no phone it was far easier to eat a messy burger and slurp at sticky milk shake. No photos, no posts, no checking, no sticky prints on my screen. Just me and the burger. The only adverse consequence was the drive-in did not collect an additional review.

What did this sunning, slurping, unrecorded morning accomplish?

Summer. The morning was all summer with no distractions or filters. He drove, I gazed out the window. We talked. I relished the wind in my face, messy hair, no make-up because unarmed, I was in no danger of submitting to a casual photograph that once posted, could become a thing. I didn't once suck in my stomach.

### 1,000 words

That Sunday afternoon, I returned to a novel in progress. Typically, it takes hours to squeeze one thousand bad, draft quality words onto the screen. But this afternoon, the writing flowed spontaneously presenting an unexpected solution to a thorny plot issue that had bedeviled me all week. It was a pleasure to write and a joy to hit that daily word requirement in about a third of my usual time. I experienced total flow and credit the morning spent sans phone, without an agenda, absent a do list or goals. At the time, I thought I was doing absolutely nothing.

Turned out it was time well invested.

## 17

## TRAVEL JOURNALS

We sunburn our lips, get eaten by invisible bugs, break our wrists while bicycling, get broadsided by an out of control kayak, lose our sunglasses in the surf, get stung by jelly fish parts (the detached flotsam of jelly fish can still sting and leave a brown strips on your cranky child). We wake to tropical rain that is so hard it sets off car alarms. We spend the night in the cold, dirty JFK terminal with our elderly mother. All captured not with photos but though travel journals.

I travel light, a single carry-on bag, one large purse and a journal.

### WHY A TRAVEL JOURNAL

Like your diary, a journal gives you something sensational to read on the train. A journal can make you mysterious. Other travelers will ask what are you writing? You can just smile and scribble away recording their questions, making up your own crazy answers.

. . .

## Capture stories that you can't photograph

Adversity makes for the best stories once you have your own bed. You can't easily photograph the experience of being lost in a foreign city, or the glorious moment you looked up and felt the enormity and opulence of Versailles. A journal is about feelings and impressions and even sketches. We are accustomed to photographing everything, but that is just one out of five senses, the more senses you engage, the more you will remember.

## Travel Journal Prompts

Contrast what you expect with what you find. I like to paste the optimistic ads or the tour descriptions of what we will see, what we will do, then annotate that description with what actually happened. Did I feel transformed by watching the sunset from the top of the crumbling temple? Or was the cautious descent down uneven building stones minutes head of a large boisterous Japanese tour group more memorable? I did not photograph my horrified face when I discovered that my mother and I were assigned a hotel room with only one queen size bed. I did write down the sympathetic exchange with the hotel clerk when I explained my problem in English, and she responded in Arabic that she understood completely and switched our room to one with two beds.

## Write what you hear

Record conversations on the street. Pause and listen to street musicians. Yes, you can certainly record them on your phone, I would argue that the experience is not the same. Notes the conversation with your Thai tour guide who lamented that she wanted elections just like in the US and you shook your head and assured her that she did not.

. . .

#### COLLECT

Rescue interesting napkins, or signs or menus or wine labels. I tear apart the museum brochure to highlight the art or the gallery I liked the best.

Grab the restaurant or hotel business card. Paste it into your journal and make quick notes on what you loved, what sucked, what would make a great poem. Bonus, if you are lost in a new city, show the card to the taxi driver – home.

The journal doesn't need to be filled with long essays. A postcard or the cookie wrapper coupled with a few comments can be one of the best triggers you have to remind you of a wonderful time and place.

#### STORIES unsuitable for a photograph

During our first night in St. Petersburg, the beginning of a three-week trip during which I would be rooming with my mother, I discovered that her travel alarm clock ticked. I am a light sleeper. Tick. It is still bright outside. Tock. I am jet lagged. Tick.

I considered my options. Tick. Weighed them. Tock. As best. Tick. As my brain could. Tock. At 3:00 AM my mother suddenly came to and ripped open the hotel curtains exclaiming "It's still light!"

Thank you for that update. Tick, tick, tick.

Three. Tick. Weeks. Tock.

The clock interrupts its ticking only to sound the alarm. I lay in bed contemplating the full-on afternoon feel of dawn in a June with no night, again, something I've always wanted to experience, thrilled about this opportunity. Tick. I ended up spending most of my first White Night working, tick, on being really, tick, really, tick, Zen.

It. Was. Not. Working.

My mother slowly rises. The alarm beeps. I contemplate the folly of sharing a room but I'm the free plus one charged with helping my mother manage such a trip in the first place. It's my job. Tock.

The beeps increase in volume and intensity as she fumbles for the off button on the back of the clock.

I closed my eyes and weighed the benefits of travel against the ticking clock.

A string of curses. A square, plastic item hits the floor and skitters under the bed.

"Damn, damn, damn!" Mom exclaims. "I dropped the clock then accidentally kicked it under the bed."

I stay very still.

She retrieves the clock and examines it.

"I think it's broken."

Prayers are answered at the oddest times. I expressed great sorrow for her loss and proceeded to cheerfully record the story in my journal. The words – *Broke Clock* take up two pages.

## Why a hard copy journal is as necessary as a computer or iPad.

Ask me about France, I will describe the light, the delight of Arles, which I have always wanted to visit. I will enthusiastically exclaim over the whole of Provence. I will describe the mussel lunch in Havre and our outing to Monet's garden - packed with tourists and the barn-like gift shop packed with 83 decorative items all covered with blue and purple water lilies.

What I will forget is to mention that on the second day of this two-week river cruise, I injured my wrist. I decided it was a sprain and refused to make a scene and just carried on with the trip. Of course, I couldn't carry much, but on this trip, I was accompanied by my husband and friends to help with both the heavy lifting as well as mom.

France is an excellent country in which to self-medicate. I discovered the efficacy of EU produced Ibuprofen that for some reason was more effective than the same OTC at home (saved the package in my journal). I began every evening with a bag of ice for the wrist and a martini for me.

What does this have to do with a journal? I am right-handed and fortunately injured my left wrist. What I couldn't do well was type, so the computer I packed did me little good (check email, upload photos, all that, but writing?). Gripping my phone to take photos was uncomfortable and I worried about dropping it. But I could write with my right hand, I could make notes anywhere. Armed (so to speak) with a paper journal, my morning routine, coffee and journaling wedged on our tiny private balcony, was not disrupted in the least. I did not lose a minute of the trip because of my fall and managed to do whatever I wanted since a person does not need her left hand on a hike through the vineyards.

When I returned home, the Kaiser staff informed me that no, it was not just a sprain. I had fractured my wrist in three places and what the hell? For two hours I was the baddest patient in the wing.

## 18

## BEAT THE HOLIDAYS BLUES

There is a specific time of year when my journal is critical for keeping me emotionally afloat and even sane: the holidays.

I am amused that when friends or acquaintances discuss the holidays, their opening questions include "Did you survive the holidays?"

Survive. A worthy topic for many ten-minute writes. Let's say you did indeed survive the holidays and its finally January (which I love, but that's likely because I live in California and the weather is surprisingly mild in January). January: post-holiday stress syndrome, land of optimistic resolutions. Not to be confused with February, the celebration of failed resolutions coupled with too much chocolate that way back on January first you resolved to give up.

As much as survival is good, even laudable. Perhaps since we now learned all these wonderful journaling skills, we can create and write about holiday strategies that can expand survival into pleasure and joy.

Rather than chugging egg nog and holding a contest on who can cram the most peppermint bark into their mouth (great contest, I may try that next year), journal about what frustrates you during the holidays and of course, what you can change.

- Crowds
- Making the damn holiday punch
- Drunk relatives
- Drunk spouses
- Expensive gifts
- Messy trees
- Messy children
- Composing the family newsletter
- Santa
- Malls
- Sending cards
- Sales
- Untangling the tree lights
- Stringing lights on the roof
- Long waits in the emergency room lobby

Now write out what you loved, especially immediately after the holidays, since hindsight is more fun and occasionally more accurate:

- Snow
- Receiving cards
- Reading family newsletters
- The cozy nights by the fire
- Eating comfort food
- Baking
- Binging on insipid holiday themed films
- Acknowledging friends
- Gathering family
- Hiking or snowshoeing in the woods

- Finding the perfect gift

Holidays are about childhood and disremembered events, love and gifts. What do you remember?

- The favorite gifts
- The favorite holiday films and cartoons
- A special outfit
- The Nutcracker
- A favorite relative
- The Christmas tree
- Favorite food
- The creche on the mantle

Write for ten minutes about each. What is there to say about Santa? A lot if you start really focusing on the jolly fellow. Write about your own experience, or that of your kids or siblings

Do you still believe in Santa?

Did you sit on his lap at the mall every year until well into your twenties?

Did your children cry in his lap?

Did you?

Are you disturbed by the necessity of believing?

### Favorites

Are there traditions you love that feed your soul?

Are there traditions you have grown to hate because they are so much trouble (looking at you Elf on the Shelf)?

Make a tradition list. Pro and Con. After listing those necessary to dos and rituals, evaluate them against what you really, really love to do.

Write about the joy of searching for the perfect tree at the Christmas tree farm. Is it still joyful?

Write about filling the stockings.

Trimming the tree

Drinking hot coco.

With brandy.

### How holidays can get out of hand.

For years part of our holiday tradition was to drive to a local tree farm and hunt for the perfect tree. It was very jolly with the boys brandishing saws and smacking each other with soaking wet tree branches while my husband wiggled in the mud under the perfect tree awkwardly sawing away at the trunk while yelling at the boys to get out of the way. I helped by not spilling my coffee.

Who could resist the joy of shaking the tree, securing the tree to the roof rack, driving the tree home, shaking it off again, vacuuming up about ten thousand pine needles as the tree is squeezed through the front door and picking off the ants and bugs?

Finished with their work, my husband disappeared, the boys disappeared and the only family member who kept me company while I strung the lights and hung the ornaments was the dog. And she was just there for the tinsel which did make it easier to pick up after her in the dark yard.

When our children left home, my husband and I realized that without the joy of chasing after small boys running with sharp objects, hunting, cutting and dragging a tree around in the December wet was a chore. We switched to purchasing a perfectly nice tree at a nearby tree lot. Once we moved to a smaller home, we went all the way and bough a fake Costco tree, complete with pre-attached lights (my request).

Suddenly a project that took the better part of Sunday,

took just ten minutes. The Platonic idea of holiday tree is still intact, just the mechanics changed. All this manifested because of my endless lists in my journal. I learned the only feature of tree hunting I really enjoyed was the mood perserving stop at Starbucks.

Journal about what would happen if you stopped doing what the family considers a sacrosanct tradition.

What if you did not write, proof, print and mail a holiday newsletter?

What if you skipped the tree?

Ate Chinese on Christmas day?

Hiked instead of shopped?

Shopped instead of hiked?

Journal about bailing from all the job and obligations you don't want to do. Journal about how it would feel to stop doing something. What are the repercussions? If you want to change the situation, journal about what would happen, what you want to happen, and play out that scene.

**Get out of Dodge**

Journal about leaving town. Not everyone can just jet to Belize for a scuba themed Thanksgiving but write about the trip anyway. What would you do? What would you pack? If you imagine the trip vividly and in enough detail: the preparations, the flights, the connections, the fact that you dislike scuba diving, it may help you be happier at home. We love to snuggle before a fire happy we are not freezing in a snowbound traffic jam.

### NOTES FOR NEXT Year

Transfer all the dos, don't, and favorite traditions into your journal and save it in a file marked Next Year. By February you'll have forgotten all the survival techniques for the holiday, so make sure you place the holiday file so come November, you find it.

Journaling about the holidays has enormous benefits. For me, journaling helped give me a better sense of control and some peace about an event that for years I started to worry about in July.

## 19
# HOW TO GAME DIFFICULT TASKS

One of the more challenging jobs for writers and artists is managing the boring bits. Tedious work can look like editing, it can look like promotion, it can look like social media, it can look like displays, meetings, fundraising and gallery hanging. No matter our passion and job, there are inescapable jobs that are always tedious and boring.

Since often we often can't afford to outsource jobs we dislike, we need to find a way to get through the process. Heck even begin.

### Productivity Hack

Start with a basic paper calendar, one month on a single page.

Estimate when the project should be finished, really finished.

Circle that date on the calendar.

In this example I'll use editing since that is my worst

event. I estimate the day I want to finish and mark it on the calendar. In this example let's say the last day of the month.

The MS is 239 pages. I want to be finished at the end of the month. A little math, and voila, my goal is to review and correct 12 pages a day to reach my end of the month finish deadline. (I take weekends off).

I mark off the total goal for each day - Monday, finish 12 pages. Tuesday, finish 24 pages, etc.

This approach does the Bullet Journal job of setting up the goal and then breaking down the goal to create doable action items. Easy.

I create these calendars whenever I'm overwhelmed by a task. Writing down the minimum number needed for success accomplishes the biggest challenge - starting.

Not so crazy, and not anything you can't find on Pinterest. Except I use a hack.

Let's say the calendar is created on a Thursday so I can start the next week - Monday, ready to conquer and launch into this daunting task.

I take a look at my manuscript and can't resist. I start editing. I finish off ten pages on Thursday, and feeling pretty smug, finish another 9 on Friday.

This means by Monday, the official start day, I'm already ahead by 19 pages.

Monday I have two choices: take the day off or keep going and blow out Monday's goal.

I always choose to blow out Monday's goal. Even if I edit the established minimum pages, by the end of the day, Monday, I will have almost reached Wednesday's goal. I decide to reach Wednesday's goal on Monday as well. I am stoked. I just succeeded beyond the requirements (and if the task was particularly impossible, my wildest dreams) of my schedule.

I just cheated on my own game.

Sometimes I re-calculate and either reduce the number of pages I need to finish to reach the end of the month deadline or I continue to do more than required. I work to exceed each day's deadline, racking up pages and points. This overachieving is exciting and satisfying and gets me through a whole week of work.

By week two, I'm over it.

To keep the momentum and motivation, I now inch the finish date forward.

Reasonably, what is the difference between finishing a book edit on a Wednesday rather than on Friday? Sure, I'll be done with an onerous task, but if I'm honest: whatever. To keep the game moving, I now invent incentives for early completion.

I create rewards of escalating value. Finish a day ahead of the deadline - win a new hard back book.

Finish two days ahead of deadline - book a massage.

Finish a week ahead of the deadline? Day at the beach.

I do not promise rewards of food or drink, fat and finished is not a good goal.

Follow through is a critical feature of this game. While I cheat at the word counts, I do not cheat the reward system. My subconscious remembers everything, so if I work at a frenzied pace so I can earn a new book, then withhold that prize, the next time I try this exercise, I'll experience more resistance than a cat on a leash.

A student used this method to set up a much-delayed yard sale. He was delighted to report back that cheating at his own game worked, and the yard sale was not only a success, more importantly, it was finished!

Part of the fun of this hack is crushing your own set goals. Be good to yourself and keep your own promises not just for the game, but forever. May the odds ever be in your favor. And they will be if you cheat.

# ACKNOWLEDGMENTS

Thank you to my students at Sierra College who helped make this book by trying out the techniques and giving me feedback.

## ABOUT THE AUTHOR

Catharine Bramkamp is a professional writing coach, bringing her clients from idea to published book to promotion. She produced 200 episodes of the writing podcast, Newbie Writers Podcast and has written 20 novels including 5 books on writing. Her poetry has been included in over a dozen anthologies including the poetry chapbook *Ammonia Sunrise* by Finishing Line Press. She served as the editor for Redwood Writer's first poetry anthology, *And the Beats Go On*.

Her most recent books are the travel poetry collection, *A Good Time was Had By All* and the mystery novel, *After I'm Buried Alive*, available on Amazon. Please leave a review!

Visit her at www.Catharine-Bramkamp.com

Unlike Donna, if you find typos or errors, please contact me with the specific error so I can correct it and re-load the book. I appreciate the help and feedback!

## 20
## BOOKS FOR AND ABOUT JOURNALING

Creativity
    The Art Instinct - Denis Dutton
    The Art of Travel - Alain De Botton
Big Magic - Elizabeth Gilbert
Creating Time - Market Makridakis
Trust the Process - Shaun McNiff
Succulent Wild Love - SARK
Steal Like an Artist - Austin Kleon
Writing the Wave - Elizabeth Ayres
Writing Down the Bones - Natalie Goldberg
Wild Minds - Natalie Goldberg

### Journaling

The Artist Way - Julia Cameron
Fire up your Writing Brain - Susan Reynolds
The Journal Writing Superpower Secret - Michael Forest
The Journal Workshop - Ira Progoff
Journal to the self - Kathleen Adams
Journey of Memoir - Linda Joy Myers

Journaling: How to Write Journal in a Way that Improves Every Aspect of Your Life - Kyial Robinson

Keep a Journal: the Basics - Matt Briggs

Let it Out: A journey Through Journaling - Katie Dalebout

Life on Purpose - Victor Strachey

Opening Up by Writing it Down - James Pennebaker and Joshua Smyth

Reclaim Your Creative Soul - Crissi Langwell

Wild ideas - Cathy Wild

Write Free, Attracting the Creative Life - Rebecca Lawton and Jordan Rosenfeld

Your Brain on Ink - Deborah Ross and Kathleen Adams

Your Next Big Thing - Ben Michaelis

**BOOKS ON WRITING by famous authors**

A Writer' Diary – Woolf

A Room of One's Own - Woolf

On Writing – Steven King

Steering the Craft – Ursula K Le Guin

The Writing of Fiction - Edith Wharton

Write Away – Elizabeth George

Writing a Woman's Life – Carolyn Heilbrun

Zen in the Art of Writing – Ray Bradbury

## Books on Writing by Newbie Writers Podcast guests

Blog your Book – Nina Amir
Don't Write Like You Talk – Catharine Bramkamp
Shoot Your Novel & The 12 Pillars of Writing - CS Lakin
You've Got a Book in You - Elizabeth Sims

## Some current favorites

The Creativity Book – Eric Maisel
Wonderbook, The Illustrated Guide to Creating Imaginative Fiction - Jeff Vandermeer
Writing Away - Lavinia Spalding
Writing the Life Poetic – Sage Cohen
Writing Wild – Tina Welling

www.ingramcontent.com/pod-product-compliance
Lightning Source LLC
LaVergne TN
LVHW051603080426
835510LV00020B/3114